Italy

Everything You Need to Know

Introduction to Italy 6

A Brief History: From Ancient Rome to Modern Italy 8

The Roman Empire: Foundations of Western Civilization 11

The Renaissance: Italy's Golden Age 14

Unification of Italy: Risorgimento and National Identity 17

Italy in World Wars: A Nation Divided 20

Italian Geography: From Alps to Mediterranean 23

Italian Wildlife: Fauna and Flora of the Peninsula 26

Italian Cuisine: A Gastronomic Journey 28

Famous Italian Dishes: Pizza, Pasta, and More 31

Wine and Olive Oil: Italy's Liquid Gold 34

Art and Architecture: Italy's Cultural Treasures 37

The Vatican City: Spiritual Heart of Catholicism 40

Italian Fashion: From Milan Runways to Global Trends 42

Italian Music: Opera, Classical, and Modern 45

The Italian Language: La Dolce Lingua 48

Italian Literature: From Dante to Calvino 51

Italian Cinema: Neorealism to Contemporary Masterpieces 54

Italian Festivals and Traditions: Celebrating Life Italian Style 56

La Dolce Vita: Italian Way of Life 58

Rome: The Eternal City 60

Florence: Cradle of the Renaissance 62

Venice: City of Canals and Romance 65

Milan: Fashion Capital of the World 68

Naples: Gateway to Southern Italy 70

Turin: Industrial Heartland and Chocolate Capital 72

Genoa: Birthplace of Christopher Columbus 75

Palermo: Jewel of Sicily 77

Bologna: Gastronomic Delights and Academic Hub 79

Verona: City of Romeo and Juliet 82

Pisa: Beyond the Leaning Tower 84

Siena: Home of the Palio Horse Race 87

Pompeii and Herculaneum: Cities Frozen in Time 89

Cinque Terre: Coastal Charm and Colorful Villages 91

Amalfi Coast: Cliffside Beauty and Mediterranean Bliss 93

Capri: Island Paradise in the Tyrrhenian Sea 95

The Italian Alps: Majestic Mountains and Alpine Adventures 97

Italian Lakes: Tranquility and Natural Splendor 99

Tuscany: Rolling Hills and Chianti Vineyards 101

Umbria: Italy's Green Heart 103

Sicily: Mediterranean Melting Pot 105

The Italian Riviera: Sun, Sea, and Style 107

Exploring Italy: Practical Tips for Travelers 109

Epilogue 112

5

Introduction to Italy

Italy, the boot-shaped peninsula nestled in the heart of the Mediterranean, is a land of rich history, vibrant culture, and breathtaking landscapes. From the snow-capped peaks of the Alps in the north to the sun-kissed shores of Sicily in the south, Italy boasts a diverse tapestry of geography and heritage that has captivated travelers for centuries.

With a history spanning over two millennia, Italy has been a cradle of civilization, witnessing the rise and fall of mighty empires, the flourishing of arts and sciences, and the birth of influential movements that have shaped the course of human history. From the glory days of the Roman Empire to the cultural renaissance of the Renaissance period, Italy has left an indelible mark on the world stage.

But Italy's allure extends beyond its storied past. It is a country of contrasts, where ancient ruins stand side by side with modern marvels, where centuries-old traditions blend seamlessly with contemporary trends. From bustling metropolises like Rome, Milan, and Naples to charming villages tucked away in the countryside, Italy offers a diverse range of experiences to suit every traveler's taste.

One of Italy's greatest treasures is its cuisine, celebrated the world over for its simplicity, freshness, and flavor. From the iconic pasta dishes of the south to the hearty risottos of the north, Italian food is a feast for the senses, inviting you to savor each bite and indulge in the pleasures of the table. And let's not forget about the wine – Italy is home to some of the world's finest vineyards, producing an array of varietals that delight wine enthusiasts from across the globe.

But Italy is more than just a feast for the senses – it is also a land of unparalleled natural beauty. From the rugged coastline of the Amalfi Coast to the rolling hills of Tuscany, from the pristine lakes of the Italian Alps to the verdant valleys of Umbria, Italy's landscapes are as diverse as they are breathtaking. Whether you're hiking in the mountains, sunbathing on the beach, or exploring ancient ruins, Italy offers endless opportunities for adventure and discovery.

In this book, we will take you on a journey through the heart and soul of Italy, exploring its rich history, vibrant culture, and stunning landscapes. From the bustling streets of Rome to the tranquil vineyards of Piedmont, from the iconic landmarks of Venice to the hidden gems of the Italian Riviera, we will introduce you to the sights, sounds, and flavors of this captivating country. So sit back, relax, and prepare to be enchanted by the magic of Italy. Buon viaggio!

A Brief History: From Ancient Rome to Modern Italy

Italy's history is a tapestry woven with threads of triumph and tragedy, spanning millennia and shaping the course of Western civilization. It all began with the ancient Romans, whose legacy still echoes in the ruins of grand amphitheaters, towering aqueducts, and majestic temples scattered across the Italian landscape. Founded in 753 BC, Rome grew from a small settlement on the banks of the Tiber River into a mighty empire that stretched from Britain to the Middle East, dominating the known world for centuries.

Under the rule of emperors like Julius Caesar, Augustus, and Trajan, Rome reached its zenith, ushering in an era of unprecedented prosperity and cultural achievement. The Pax Romana, or Roman Peace, brought stability and security to the empire, facilitating trade, commerce, and the spread of ideas. But Rome's golden age was not to last – internal strife, external threats, and economic decline eventually led to the empire's downfall in the 5th century AD.

With the fall of Rome came the beginning of the Dark Ages, a period of chaos and upheaval marked by barbarian invasions, feudalism, and the rise of Christianity. Italy, once the heart of a mighty empire, became a patchwork of warring city-states and petty kingdoms, each vying for power and influence. But out of this turmoil emerged the seeds of a cultural revival – the Renaissance.

Beginning in the 14th century, the Renaissance saw a rebirth of interest in art, literature, science, and philosophy, fueled by a newfound spirit of humanism and a rediscovery of the classical past. Italian city-states like Florence, Venice, and Rome became centers of innovation and creativity, attracting artists, scholars, and thinkers from across Europe. Figures like Leonardo da Vinci, Michelangelo, and Galileo Galilei left an indelible mark on history, their contributions laying the groundwork for the modern world.

But Italy's journey towards nationhood was not without its challenges. For centuries, the Italian peninsula remained fragmented and divided, ruled by foreign powers and torn apart by internal strife. It was not until the 19th century that the dream of a unified Italy began to take shape, spurred on by the ideals of nationalism and the desire for independence.

Led by visionaries like Giuseppe Garibaldi and Count Camillo di Cavour, Italy embarked on a quest for unification known as the Risorgimento, or Resurgence. Through a series of wars, revolutions, and diplomatic maneuvers, the various states and territories of Italy were brought together under the banner of a single nation-state in 1861, with Victor Emmanuel II crowned as its first king.

Since then, Italy has undergone a remarkable transformation, evolving from a fledgling nation into a modern industrialized state. From the turmoil of two world wars to the economic boom of the post-war years, Italy has faced its share of challenges and triumphs, shaping the identity of its people and the destiny of its nation.

Today, Italy stands as a beacon of culture, heritage, and innovation, attracting millions of visitors each year with its timeless beauty and timeless charm. From the ancient ruins of Rome to the fashion boutiques of Milan, from the vineyards of Tuscany to the canals of Venice, Italy continues to inspire and enchant, a living testament to the enduring spirit of its people and the enduring legacy of its past.

The Roman Empire: Foundations of Western Civilization

The Roman Empire stands as one of the most influential civilizations in history, laying the groundwork for much of Western civilization as we know it today. Originating from the small city-state of Rome, located in present-day Italy, the empire expanded over the course of centuries to encompass vast territories across Europe, North Africa, and the Middle East.

Founded in 753 BC, according to legend, Rome began as a humble village on the banks of the Tiber River. Over time, it grew into a powerful republic, characterized by a system of government in which elected officials governed on behalf of the people. The Roman Republic thrived for centuries, expanding its territory through conquest and diplomacy, until it was eventually replaced by the Roman Empire in 27 BC, with the ascension of Julius Caesar's grandnephew, Augustus, as the first emperor.

Under the rule of emperors like Augustus, Trajan, and Hadrian, the Roman Empire reached its zenith, encompassing over 2 million square miles and boasting a population of over 60 million people. At its height, it stretched from the British Isles in the north to the deserts of

Egypt in the south, from the Atlantic Ocean in the west to the Euphrates River in the east.

One of the greatest achievements of the Roman Empire was its system of governance and law. The Romans developed a sophisticated legal system based on principles of justice, fairness, and the rule of law, which served as a model for legal systems throughout the world. They also built an extensive network of roads, bridges, and aqueducts, connecting the far reaches of the empire and facilitating trade, commerce, and communication.

But perhaps the most enduring legacy of the Roman Empire is its contributions to art, architecture, and culture. The Romans were master builders, constructing grand monuments like the Colosseum, the Pantheon, and the Forum, which still stand as testaments to their ingenuity and engineering prowess. They also made significant advances in literature, philosophy, and the arts, producing such luminaries as Virgil, Cicero, and Seneca.

But for all its achievements, the Roman Empire was not without its flaws. Its vast size and diverse population made it difficult to govern effectively, leading to corruption, inequality, and social unrest. Over time, internal strife, external threats, and economic decline took their toll, leading to the eventual collapse of the Western Roman Empire in 476 AD.

Despite its fall, the legacy of the Roman Empire endured, shaping the course of Western civilization for centuries to come. Its language, Latin, evolved into the Romance languages spoken across Europe today. Its legal and political institutions laid the groundwork for modern democracy and governance. And its art, architecture, and culture continue to inspire and captivate people around the world, a testament to the enduring power and influence of Rome.

The Renaissance: Italy's Golden Age

The Renaissance stands as one of the most pivotal periods in Italy's history, marking a golden age of creativity, innovation, and cultural revival. Emerging in the 14th century, the Renaissance was a time of rebirth, as Italy experienced a resurgence of interest in art, literature, science, and philosophy. It was a period of enlightenment, characterized by a newfound spirit of humanism and a reawakening of the classical past.

Italian city-states like Florence, Venice, and Rome became vibrant centers of intellectual and artistic activity, attracting scholars, artists, and thinkers from across Europe. Figures like Leonardo da Vinci, Michelangelo, and Raphael flourished during this time, producing some of the greatest masterpieces of Western art. From the sublime beauty of the Sistine Chapel ceiling to the timeless elegance of Botticelli's "Birth of Venus," the art of the Renaissance continues to captivate and inspire people around the world.

But the Renaissance was not just a time of artistic achievement – it was also a period of scientific and intellectual revolution. Scholars like Galileo Galilei, Nicolaus Copernicus, and Johannes Kepler challenged long-held beliefs about the nature of the universe, paving the way for modern science and the scientific method. Meanwhile, writers like Dante Alighieri, Petrarch, and Giovanni Boccaccio revitalized literature with their works, laying the foundations for modern literature and poetry.

One of the driving forces behind the Renaissance was the rise of humanism, a philosophical movement that emphasized the importance of human reason, dignity, and potential. Humanists sought to revive the study of classical literature, philosophy, and art, believing that these disciplines held the key to understanding the world and achieving personal fulfillment. Their ideas spread rapidly throughout Italy and beyond, shaping the intellectual landscape of Europe for centuries to come.

The Renaissance also saw the emergence of powerful patrons, such as the Medici family of Florence, who provided financial support and encouragement to artists, scholars, and architects. Through their patronage, they helped to foster an environment of creativity and innovation, enabling some of the greatest achievements of the Renaissance to flourish.

But for all its brilliance, the Renaissance was not without its contradictions. While it celebrated the beauty and potential of humanity, it also perpetuated social inequalities and injustices, particularly against women and marginalized groups. Moreover, the wealth and power amassed by the ruling elite often came at the expense of the common people, leading to social unrest and political instability.

Despite these challenges, the legacy of the Renaissance endures, shaping the course of Western civilization and influencing every aspect of modern life. Its art, literature, and philosophy continue to inspire and challenge us, reminding us of the power of human creativity and the enduring quest for knowledge and truth. In many ways, the Renaissance represents the pinnacle of Italy's cultural and intellectual achievements, a shining beacon of hope and inspiration for generations to come.

Unification of Italy: Risorgimento and National Identity

The Unification of Italy, known as the Risorgimento, was a transformative period in the country's history, marking the culmination of centuries-long struggles for independence and unity. Prior to the 19th century, Italy was a patchwork of independent states, duchies, and kingdoms, ruled by foreign powers and divided along linguistic, cultural, and political lines. But as the winds of nationalism swept across Europe in the wake of the French Revolution, the people of Italy began to dream of a unified nation-state of their own.

The Risorgimento was fueled by a sense of national identity and a desire for self-determination, as Italians sought to overthrow foreign rule and establish a united Italy. The movement gained momentum in the early 19th century, inspired by the ideals of liberty, equality, and fraternity espoused by revolutionary thinkers like Giuseppe Mazzini and Giuseppe Garibaldi. These visionary leaders called for the overthrow of oppressive regimes and the creation of a republic based on democratic principles.

But the road to unification was long and arduous, fraught with internal divisions, external threats, and political intrigue. The Risorgimento saw numerous uprisings, revolutions, and wars, as Italian patriots fought valiantly against foreign invaders and oppressive rulers. One of the key figures in the struggle for unification was Count Camillo di Cavour, the prime minister of the Kingdom of Piedmont-Sardinia, who skillfully maneuvered diplomatic alliances and military campaigns to bring about the downfall of the old order.

The Risorgimento reached its climax in 1861, when the Kingdom of Italy was officially proclaimed, with Victor Emmanuel II crowned as its first king. But the struggle for unification was far from over – large swathes of territory remained under foreign control, including the Papal States in central Italy and the Kingdom of the Two Sicilies in the south. It was not until 1870, with the capture of Rome by Italian forces, that the dream of a united Italy was finally realized.

The Unification of Italy was a triumph of determination, courage, and sacrifice, as ordinary Italians from all walks of life came together to forge a new nation out of the ashes of the old. But it was also a complex and contentious process, marked by compromises, betrayals, and unresolved tensions. The question of regional autonomy, the role of the Catholic Church, and the treatment of minority groups all posed challenges to the fledgling nation, which would continue to shape Italy's identity and politics for generations to come.

Despite these challenges, the Risorgimento left an indelible mark on the Italian psyche, instilling a sense of national pride and solidarity that endures to this day. The ideals of liberty, equality, and fraternity that fueled the movement continue to inspire Italians as they strive to build a more just, inclusive, and prosperous society. The Unification of Italy was not just a political event – it was a defining moment in the nation's history, shaping its destiny and shaping the course of Western civilization.

Italy in World Wars: A Nation Divided

Italy's involvement in the World Wars left a lasting impact on the nation, as it grappled with internal divisions and external pressures that tested its unity and resilience. In World War I, Italy initially remained neutral, but in 1915, it entered the conflict on the side of the Allies, motivated by territorial ambitions and promises of territorial gains. The Italian front, characterized by grueling trench warfare in the mountainous terrain of the Alps, proved to be one of the deadliest theaters of the war, claiming the lives of hundreds of thousands of soldiers on both sides.

The aftermath of World War I brought significant political and social upheaval to Italy, as the country struggled to cope with the economic devastation and social dislocation wrought by the conflict. The rise of fascism, led by Benito Mussolini, promised stability and renewal, tapping into widespread discontent and disillusionment with the political establishment. In 1922, Mussolini marched on Rome with his Blackshirts, a paramilitary force, and seized power, establishing a dictatorship that would rule Italy for the next two decades.

Under Mussolini's rule, Italy embarked on a program of aggressive expansionism, seeking to restore the glory of the Roman Empire and assert its dominance in the Mediterranean region. In 1935, Italy invaded Ethiopia, sparking international condemnation and sanctions from the League of Nations. Despite these setbacks, Mussolini's popularity soared at home, as he promised to make Italy great again and restore its former glory.

But Italy's alliance with Nazi Germany in World War II would prove to be its undoing. In 1940, Mussolini declared war on the Allies, hoping to capitalize on Germany's military successes and expand Italy's territorial holdings. However, the Italian military proved ill-prepared and poorly equipped for the rigors of modern warfare, suffering humiliating defeats in North Africa, the Balkans, and the Mediterranean.

By 1943, with the Allied invasion of Sicily, Italy's position in the war became untenable. Mussolini was ousted from power and arrested by his own government, and Italy signed an armistice with the Allies, effectively ending its participation in the war. But the country remained deeply divided – while some Italians welcomed the end of fascism and embraced the Allied cause, others remained loyal to Mussolini and his fascist ideology, forming the Italian Social Republic in northern Italy and continuing to fight alongside the Germans until the bitter end.

The legacy of Italy's involvement in the World Wars is complex and contentious, with lingering debates and controversies about the nation's role and responsibility in the conflicts. But one thing is clear – the experience of war left an indelible mark on the Italian psyche, shaping the nation's identity and politics for generations to come. Italy emerged from the World Wars battered and bruised, but also resilient and determined to rebuild and move forward as a united and democratic nation.

Italian Geography: From Alps to Mediterranean

Italy's geography is as diverse as it is beautiful, encompassing a wide range of landscapes and ecosystems that stretch from the towering peaks of the Alps in the north to the sun-drenched shores of the Mediterranean in the south. In the north, the Italian Alps form a natural barrier between Italy and the rest of Europe, with majestic peaks reaching heights of over 15,000 feet. The Alps are a haven for outdoor enthusiasts, offering opportunities for hiking, skiing, and mountaineering amidst breathtaking scenery.

South of the Alps lies the fertile Po Valley, Italy's largest plain and its agricultural heartland. Fed by the waters of the Po River and its tributaries, the valley is home to lush vineyards, fertile farmland, and bustling cities like Milan, Turin, and Bologna. The Po Valley is also a major industrial center, with factories and manufacturing facilities dotting the landscape.

To the west of the Po Valley lies the Ligurian coast, a rugged stretch of coastline characterized by steep cliffs, hidden coves, and picturesque fishing villages. The region is famous for its colorful towns like Cinque Terre and Portofino, which attract visitors with their charm and beauty. The Ligurian coast is also known for its cuisine, particularly its seafood dishes and pesto sauce.

Moving south along the coast, we come to Tuscany, one of Italy's most iconic regions. Tuscany is renowned for its rolling hills, vineyards, and olive groves, as well as its historic cities like Florence, Siena, and Pisa. The region's Renaissance art and architecture, delicious cuisine, and picturesque countryside make it a favorite destination for travelers from around the world.

Continuing south, we reach the Bay of Naples, home to the bustling city of Naples and the stunning Amalfi Coast. The Amalfi Coast is famous for its dramatic cliffs, colorful villages, and crystal-clear waters, making it a popular destination for beachgoers and romantics alike. Nearby, the ancient city of Pompeii offers a fascinating glimpse into Italy's past, with its well-preserved ruins and artifacts.

Further south, we find the island of Sicily, separated from the mainland by the Strait of Messina. Sicily boasts a diverse landscape, with rugged mountains, fertile plains, and sandy beaches. The island is rich in history and culture, with ancient Greek temples, Roman ruins, and Arab-Norman architecture dotting the landscape.

Sicily is also known for its delicious cuisine, which blends Italian, Greek, Arabic, and Spanish influences.

Finally, in the far south of Italy, we find the island of Sardinia, known for its pristine beaches, rugged interior, and unique culture. Sardinia is home to ancient nuraghe stone structures, prehistoric villages, and traditional festivals that celebrate the island's rich heritage.

From north to south, Italy's geography is a testament to the country's diversity and beauty, offering something for everyone to explore and enjoy. Whether you're drawn to the snow-capped peaks of the Alps, the sun-drenched beaches of the Mediterranean, or the historic cities and charming villages that dot the landscape, Italy has something to offer every traveler.

Italian Wildlife: Fauna and Flora of the Peninsula

Italy's wildlife is as diverse as its landscapes, with a rich tapestry of fauna and flora that spans from the snow-capped peaks of the Alps to the sun-drenched shores of the Mediterranean. In the mountainous regions of the north, you'll find a variety of alpine species, including ibex, chamois, and marmots, adapted to the harsh conditions of high altitudes. The dense forests of the Apennine Mountains are home to wolves, bears, and wild boars, as well as a variety of bird species such as golden eagles, peregrine falcons, and hoopoes.

Moving down to the plains and valleys of the Po Valley, you'll encounter a different array of wildlife, including deer, foxes, and hares, as well as numerous species of birds, reptiles, and amphibians. The wetlands and marshes of the Po Delta are important habitats for migratory birds, such as herons, egrets, and flamingos, which flock to the region in large numbers during the winter months.

Along the coastlines of Italy, you'll find a wealth of marine life, from dolphins and seals to sea turtles and colorful fish. The waters of the Mediterranean are teeming with biodiversity, supporting vibrant coral reefs, seagrass beds, and kelp forests. The Ligurian Sea is home to one of the largest populations of bottlenose dolphins in Europe, while the Tyrrhenian Sea is known for its rich diversity of marine mammals, including sperm whales and fin whales.

In terms of flora, Italy boasts a wide variety of plant species, ranging from alpine meadows and coniferous forests in the north to Mediterranean scrubland and olive groves in the south. The hillsides of Tuscany are covered in vineyards and olive orchards, while the rolling countryside of Umbria is blanketed in fields of sunflowers and wheat. Along the coastlines, you'll find fragrant citrus groves, colorful bougainvillea, and towering palm trees, creating a lush and vibrant landscape that is quintessentially Mediterranean.

Italy's biodiversity is not only important for its ecological value but also for its cultural significance. Many of Italy's national parks and nature reserves are home to ancient forests, sacred groves, and sacred mountains that hold deep spiritual and cultural significance for the people of Italy. Protecting these natural treasures is essential for preserving Italy's rich biodiversity and ensuring that future generations can continue to enjoy the beauty and wonder of the Italian countryside.

Italian Cuisine: A Gastronomic Journey

Italian cuisine is renowned worldwide for its delicious flavors, fresh ingredients, and rich culinary traditions. It's a gastronomic journey that reflects the country's diverse regional cultures and historical influences, ranging from the hearty pasta dishes of the north to the seafood delicacies of the south. At the heart of Italian cuisine is the concept of simplicity – using quality ingredients to create dishes that are both flavorful and satisfying.

Pasta is perhaps the most iconic of all Italian foods, with hundreds of shapes and varieties to choose from. In the north, you'll find hearty dishes like tagliatelle al ragù (pasta with meat sauce) and tortellini in brodo (stuffed pasta in broth), while in the south, you'll find lighter options like spaghetti alle vongole (spaghetti with clams) and orecchiette con cime di rapa (pasta with broccoli rabe). No matter where you are in Italy, you're sure to find a pasta dish that will tantalize your taste buds.

But Italian cuisine is not just about pasta – it's also about fresh, seasonal ingredients that are cooked with care and attention to detail. Italy's fertile soil and temperate climate produce an abundance of fruits, vegetables, and herbs, which form the basis of many traditional dishes. From ripe tomatoes and fragrant basil to crisp lettuce and peppery arugula, Italian cuisine celebrates the bounty of the land in all its glory.

Italy's coastline is also a rich source of inspiration for its culinary creations, with seafood playing a prominent role in many regional cuisines. In the coastal regions of Liguria and Campania, you'll find dishes like pesto alla genovese (basil pesto with pasta) and spaghetti alle cozze (spaghetti with mussels), which showcase the fresh flavors of the sea. Further south in Sicily, you'll find exotic dishes like arancini (rice balls stuffed with cheese and seafood) and caponata (a savory eggplant stew), which reflect the island's diverse cultural heritage.

Of course, no discussion of Italian cuisine would be complete without mentioning pizza – Italy's most famous export. Originating in Naples in the 18th century, pizza has become a global phenomenon, with countless variations and toppings to suit every taste. Whether you prefer a classic Margherita with tomato, mozzarella, and basil or a more adventurous combination like prosciutto and arugula, pizza is a beloved staple of Italian cuisine that has captured the hearts and stomachs of people around the world.

But perhaps the true secret to Italian cuisine's success lies not just in its delicious flavors or fresh ingredients, but in the joy and conviviality that comes with sharing a meal with loved ones. Italians take great pride in their food and consider it an integral part of their culture and identity. Whether it's a leisurely Sunday lunch with family or a festive dinner with friends, the shared experience of breaking bread together is what truly makes Italian cuisine a gastronomic journey worth savoring.

Famous Italian Dishes: Pizza, Pasta, and More

When it comes to famous Italian dishes, few can rival the popularity and ubiquity of pizza and pasta. Pizza, with its crispy crust, tangy tomato sauce, and gooey cheese, is a culinary icon beloved the world over. Originating in Naples in the 18th century, pizza was initially a simple dish enjoyed by the city's working-class residents. However, it wasn't long before pizza's delicious flavors and satisfying simplicity caught on, spreading to other parts of Italy and eventually making its way across the globe.

Today, pizza comes in countless variations, from classic Margherita and pepperoni to more exotic combinations like Hawaiian and BBQ chicken. Whether you prefer thin and crispy Roman-style pizza or thick and chewy Neapolitan-style pizza, there's a pie out there to suit every taste and preference.

But pizza is just one part of Italy's culinary repertoire – pasta is another staple that has captivated diners for centuries. Made from durum wheat flour and water, pasta is a versatile and satisfying dish that can be dressed up with a variety of sauces, meats, and vegetables. From the creamy richness of fettuccine Alfredo to the spicy kick of spaghetti arrabbiata, there's a pasta dish out there for every palate.

In addition to pizza and pasta, Italy is also famous for its other culinary delights, including risotto, gnocchi, and polenta. Risotto, a creamy rice dish cooked slowly with broth and flavored with ingredients like mushrooms, seafood, or saffron, is a favorite in the northern regions of Italy. Gnocchi, small dumplings made from potato, flour, and egg, are popular throughout the country and can be served with a variety of sauces, from tomato to pesto.

And let's not forget about polenta, a hearty cornmeal dish that originated in northern Italy and is typically served as a side dish or accompaniment to meat and cheese. Whether it's grilled, fried, or baked, polenta is a delicious and comforting addition to any meal.

Of course, no discussion of famous Italian dishes would be complete without mentioning gelato, Italy's answer to ice cream. Made with milk, sugar, and flavorings like fruit, nuts, or chocolate, gelato is known for its creamy texture and intense flavor. Whether you're strolling through the streets of Rome or lounging on the beaches of Sicily, a scoop of gelato is the perfect way to cool off and indulge your sweet tooth.

From pizza and pasta to risotto and gelato, Italy's culinary heritage is as rich and diverse as its history and culture. Whether you're dining in a Michelin-starred restaurant or enjoying a casual meal at a trattoria, you're sure to find something delicious to satisfy your cravings and leave you craving more.

Wine and Olive Oil: Italy's Liquid Gold

In Italy, wine and olive oil are not just beverages and condiments – they're a way of life. With a history dating back thousands of years, Italy's wine and olive oil industries are among the oldest and most prestigious in the world. From the rolling hills of Tuscany to the sun-drenched slopes of Sicily, Italy's diverse climate and terroir produce an astonishing array of wines and olive oils, each with its own unique characteristics and flavors.

Italy is home to over 2,000 grape varieties, making it one of the most diverse wine-producing countries on earth. From the robust reds of Piedmont to the crisp whites of Friuli-Venezia Giulia, Italian wines are celebrated for their quality, complexity, and versatility. Some of Italy's most famous wine regions include Chianti in Tuscany, Barolo in Piedmont, and Brunello di Montalcino in Umbria, each known for producing wines of exceptional quality and character.

But it's not just the wine that makes Italy special – it's also the olive oil. Italy is the world's second-largest producer of olive oil, after Spain, and its extra virgin olive oils are prized for their fruity flavor, peppery finish, and vibrant color.

From the delicate oils of Liguria to the robust oils of Puglia, Italy's olive oils come in a variety of styles and flavors, each reflecting the unique characteristics of the region in which it was produced.

The cultivation of grapes and olives has been an integral part of Italian culture for millennia, dating back to ancient times. The Etruscans, Romans, and Greeks all recognized the importance of wine and olive oil in daily life, using them for cooking, religious ceremonies, and medicinal purposes. Today, Italian wines and olive oils continue to play a central role in Italian cuisine and culture, with each region boasting its own proud traditions and techniques.

In recent years, Italian wines and olive oils have gained international acclaim, winning awards and accolades from critics and connoisseurs around the world. Italian wine exports have soared, with bottles of Barolo, Amarone, and Super Tuscan wines finding their way onto the shelves of wine shops and restaurants in every corner of the globe. Similarly, Italian olive oils have become sought-after gourmet products, prized for their superior quality and artisanal craftsmanship.

But perhaps the true beauty of Italian wine and olive oil lies not just in their taste or quality, but in the way they bring people together. Whether it's sharing a bottle of Chianti with friends over dinner or drizzling extra virgin olive oil over a crusty loaf of bread, Italian wine and olive oil have a way of enhancing life's simple pleasures and creating lasting memories. In Italy, wine and olive oil are more than just commodities – they're a way of life, a celebration of the land and the people who tend it, and a testament to the timeless beauty and bounty of Italy's countryside.

Art and Architecture: Italy's Cultural Treasures

Italy's art and architecture stand as a testament to the country's rich cultural heritage and enduring legacy. From the grandeur of ancient Rome to the exquisite beauty of the Renaissance, Italy's artistic treasures are among the most celebrated and revered in the world. The country's artistic legacy dates back thousands of years, with the ancient Romans leaving behind magnificent monuments like the Colosseum, the Pantheon, and the Forum, which continue to awe and inspire visitors to this day.

But it was during the Renaissance that Italy truly came into its own as a center of artistic innovation and creativity. In cities like Florence, Venice, and Rome, a new generation of artists, architects, and thinkers emerged, producing some of the greatest masterpieces of Western art and architecture. Figures like Leonardo da Vinci, Michelangelo, and Raphael created works that continue to captivate and inspire people around the world, from the sublime beauty of the Sistine Chapel ceiling to the timeless elegance of Botticelli's "The Birth of Venus."

The Renaissance also saw the emergence of architectural wonders like the Florence Cathedral, the Doge's Palace in Venice, and St.

Peter's Basilica in Rome, which pushed the boundaries of design and engineering and left an indelible mark on the built environment. These monumental structures, with their soaring domes, intricate facades, and graceful proportions, are a testament to the ingenuity and creativity of the architects and craftsmen who built them.

In addition to its Renaissance treasures, Italy is also home to a wealth of medieval and Baroque architecture, with charming hilltop towns, majestic castles, and ornate churches dotting the countryside. From the medieval city of Siena with its magnificent cathedral and Piazza del Campo to the Baroque splendor of Rome's Trevi Fountain and Spanish Steps, Italy's architectural heritage is as diverse as it is breathtaking.

But Italy's cultural treasures are not limited to its art and architecture – the country is also home to a wealth of museums, galleries, and cultural institutions that showcase its rich artistic heritage. From the Uffizi Gallery in Florence to the Vatican Museums in Rome, Italy's museums house some of the world's greatest art collections, featuring works by masters like Caravaggio, Titian, and Vermeer.

In recent years, Italy has also made efforts to preserve and protect its cultural heritage, with initiatives to restore and conserve historic buildings, monuments, and works of art. Organizations like UNESCO have recognized the importance of Italy's cultural treasures, designating sites like the Historic Centre of Rome, the Cathedral of Modena, and the Archaeological Area of Pompeii as World Heritage Sites, ensuring that they will be preserved for future generations to enjoy.

Overall, Italy's art and architecture are a testament to the country's enduring creativity, innovation, and cultural richness. From the grandeur of ancient Rome to the elegance of the Renaissance, Italy's cultural treasures continue to captivate and inspire people around the world, reminding us of the timeless beauty and genius of the Italian spirit.

The Vatican City: Spiritual Heart of Catholicism

The Vatican City stands as the spiritual heart of Catholicism, a tiny city-state nestled within the heart of Rome. Covering just over 100 acres, it is the smallest independent state in the world, yet its significance transcends its size. Home to the Pope, the head of the Catholic Church, the Vatican serves as the center of the Church's spiritual and administrative authority, overseeing the lives of over a billion Catholics worldwide.

The history of the Vatican can be traced back over two millennia, to the earliest days of Christianity. According to tradition, it was here, on the site of St. Peter's Basilica, that the apostle Peter was martyred and buried, making it one of the holiest sites in Christendom. Over the centuries, the Vatican grew in importance, as popes and bishops from around the world came to Rome to seek guidance and support from the Church's spiritual leaders.

In 1929, the Vatican City was established as an independent state through the Lateran Treaty between the Holy See and the Kingdom of Italy, securing the Church's sovereignty and autonomy within its own borders. Today, the Vatican is governed by the Pope, who serves as the supreme pontiff and spiritual leader of the

Catholic Church. The Pope is elected by the College of Cardinals, a group of senior bishops and clergy who gather in conclave to choose the successor to St. Peter.

The Vatican is not just a religious institution – it's also a cultural and artistic treasure trove, home to some of the world's greatest works of art and architecture. From the magnificent frescoes of the Sistine Chapel, painted by Michelangelo, to the stunning mosaics of St. Peter's Basilica, the Vatican's artistic heritage is unrivaled in its beauty and significance. The Vatican Museums, which house thousands of works of art collected by the Church over the centuries, are among the most visited museums in the world, attracting millions of visitors each year.

But perhaps the most important role of the Vatican is its spiritual mission – to spread the message of the Gospel and minister to the spiritual needs of Catholics around the world. Through its charitable works, diplomatic efforts, and pastoral outreach, the Vatican seeks to promote peace, justice, and solidarity among all people, regardless of their religious beliefs or background. In a world marked by division and conflict, the Vatican stands as a beacon of hope and unity, offering a message of love, compassion, and reconciliation to all who seek it.

Italian Fashion: From Milan Runways to Global Trends

Italian fashion has long been synonymous with luxury, sophistication, and style, setting trends and influencing the global fashion industry for decades. At the heart of Italy's fashion scene is the city of Milan, often referred to as the fashion capital of the world. Milan is home to some of the most prestigious fashion houses and designers, including Versace, Prada, Gucci, and Armani, whose runway shows and collections set the tone for the rest of the industry.

Italian fashion has its roots in the Renaissance, when Italian cities like Florence and Venice were centers of trade and commerce, attracting wealthy patrons and artisans from around the world. It was during this period that Italian tailors and craftsmen began to gain a reputation for their skill and artistry, producing exquisite garments and accessories for the nobility and elite.

In the 20th century, Italy emerged as a major player in the global fashion industry, thanks in large part to the efforts of designers like Giorgio Armani and Miuccia Prada, who revolutionized the way people think about fashion and style. Armani's minimalist aesthetic and emphasis on clean lines and understated elegance helped to define modern Italian fashion, while Prada's innovative designs and avant-garde sensibility pushed the boundaries of creativity and expression.

Today, Italian fashion is known for its impeccable craftsmanship, attention to detail, and commitment to quality. Italian designers use only the finest materials and fabrics, from sumptuous silks and cashmeres to luxurious leathers and furs, ensuring that every garment is a work of art in its own right. Italian fashion houses also place a strong emphasis on innovation and creativity, constantly pushing the envelope and exploring new techniques and ideas.

But Italian fashion is not just about haute couture and high-end luxury – it's also about everyday elegance and effortless chic. Italian women are renowned for their impeccable sense of style and ability to effortlessly mix and match designer pieces with high-street finds, creating looks that are both fashionable and practical. Italian men, too, are known for their sartorial savvy, with tailored suits, crisp shirts, and polished shoes forming the foundation of their wardrobe.

In addition to its fashion designers, Italy is also home to a thriving textile and manufacturing industry, producing everything from fine fabrics and leather goods to shoes and accessories. Italian craftsmanship is revered around the world for its attention to detail and commitment to quality, with many of the country's artisans passing down their skills and techniques from generation to generation.

Overall, Italian fashion is a celebration of creativity, craftsmanship, and self-expression, reflecting the country's rich cultural heritage and innovative spirit. From the runways of Milan to the streets of Rome, Italian fashion continues to inspire and captivate people around the world, setting trends and shaping the way we dress and present ourselves to the world.

Italian Music: Opera, Classical, and Modern

Italian music holds a storied history, with contributions spanning classical, opera, and modern genres. Italy's influence in music can be traced back centuries, with the country producing some of the most renowned composers and performers in the world. One of Italy's most significant contributions to the musical world is opera, a dramatic art form that combines music, theater, and storytelling. Opera originated in Italy in the late 16th century and quickly spread throughout Europe, becoming one of the most popular forms of entertainment among the elite and aristocracy. Italian composers like Giuseppe Verdi, Giacomo Puccini, and Gioachino Rossini are among the most celebrated figures in opera, known for their lush melodies, passionate storytelling, and dramatic flair. Works like Verdi's "La Traviata," Puccini's "La Bohème," and Rossini's "The Barber of Seville" continue to captivate audiences around the world with their emotional depth and timeless beauty.

In addition to opera, Italy has a rich tradition of classical music, with composers like Antonio Vivaldi, Arcangelo Corelli, and Claudio Monteverdi making significant contributions to the genre. Vivaldi, in particular, is known for his virtuosic violin concertos, including "The Four Seasons," which remains one of the most beloved and frequently performed works in the classical repertoire. Italy's classical music heritage also extends to the realm of sacred music, with composers like Giovanni Pierluigi da Palestrina and Gregorio Allegri producing exquisite choral works for the church.

But Italy's musical legacy is not confined to the past – the country continues to be a vibrant hub of musical creativity and innovation, with a thriving modern music scene that encompasses a wide range of genres and styles. From pop and rock to hip-hop and electronic music, Italian artists are making waves both at home and abroad, with acts like Laura Pausini, Eros Ramazzotti, and Vasco Rossi achieving international success and acclaim. Italy's music festivals, including the Sanremo Music Festival and the Umbria Jazz Festival, attract thousands of music lovers from around the world each year, showcasing the best in Italian and international talent.

In recent years, Italy has also emerged as a powerhouse in the world of classical crossover music, with artists like Andrea Bocelli, Il Divo, and Sarah Brightman blending classical and pop influences to create a new and exciting musical hybrid. Bocelli, in particular, has achieved superstar status with his powerful voice and emotional performances, selling millions of albums worldwide and performing to sold-out crowds in some of the world's most prestigious venues.

Overall, Italian music is a reflection of the country's rich cultural heritage, diverse influences, and creative spirit. From the grandeur of opera to the intimacy of classical chamber music and the energy of modern pop and rock, Italy's musical tradition is as vibrant and diverse as the country itself, offering something for every listener to enjoy and appreciate.

The Italian Language: La Dolce Lingua

The Italian language, often referred to as "la dolce lingua" or "the sweet language," is a beautiful and melodic Romance language spoken by millions of people around the world. With its roots in Latin, Italian is closely related to other Romance languages such as Spanish, French, and Portuguese, but it has its own distinct characteristics and flavor that set it apart.

Italian is the official language of Italy and is spoken by the majority of the country's population, but it is also widely spoken in other parts of the world, particularly in regions with large Italian immigrant communities such as the United States, Canada, Argentina, and Australia. In addition to its native speakers, Italian is also recognized as an official language of several international organizations, including the European Union and the United Nations.

One of the most distinctive features of the Italian language is its musicality and rhythm, with words and phrases flowing smoothly and melodically off the tongue. Italian is known for its expressive gestures and facial expressions, which are often used in conjunction with speech to convey emotion and meaning. In Italian culture, communication is seen as a dynamic and interactive process, with an emphasis on warmth, intimacy, and personal connection.

Italian is also a highly phonetic language, meaning that words are pronounced as they are spelled, making it relatively easy for learners to grasp the basics of pronunciation. Unlike English, which has many irregularities and exceptions, Italian grammar is relatively straightforward, with a clear set of rules governing verb conjugation, noun gender, and sentence structure. However, like any language, Italian does have its quirks and idiosyncrasies, such as the use of double consonants and the placement of accent marks, which can sometimes trip up learners.

Italian vocabulary is rich and varied, with words and expressions borrowed from Latin, Greek, Arabic, French, and other languages. Italian cuisine, art, music, and literature have all left their mark on the language, contributing to its vibrant and diverse lexicon. Italian is also known for its poetic and lyrical quality, with many famous poets, writers, and playwrights, such as Dante Alighieri, Giovanni Boccaccio, and Giacomo Leopardi, composing works of great beauty and depth in the language.

Today, Italian remains a vital and thriving language, spoken by millions of people around the world and celebrated for its beauty, elegance, and cultural significance. Whether you're learning Italian for business, travel, or personal enrichment, immersing yourself in the language and culture of Italy is sure to be a rewarding and enriching experience. So, whether you're ordering a cappuccino in a café in Rome or exploring the streets of Florence, take the time to savor the beauty and richness of the Italian language – la dolce lingua – and discover the magic of Italy for yourself.

Italian Literature: From Dante to Calvino

Italian literature is a rich tapestry woven with the threads of history, culture, and imagination, stretching back over a thousand years. From the epic poetry of Dante Alighieri to the postmodern fiction of Italo Calvino, Italian writers have made enduring contributions to world literature, exploring themes of love, loss, redemption, and the human condition with insight and eloquence.

One of the most influential figures in Italian literature is Dante Alighieri, often referred to as the "father of the Italian language." Dante's Divine Comedy, written in the early 14th century, is widely considered one of the greatest works of literature ever written. Comprising three parts – Inferno, Purgatorio, and Paradiso – the Divine Comedy follows Dante's journey through the afterlife, exploring themes of sin, salvation, and divine justice. Dante's use of vernacular Italian, rather than Latin, helped to popularize the language and establish it as a literary medium in its own right.

Following in Dante's footsteps, Petrarch and Boccaccio, two of the greatest Italian poets of the Renaissance, made significant contributions to Italian literature with their lyric poetry and narrative prose. Petrarch, often considered the father of humanism, is best known for his sonnets dedicated to his muse, Laura, while Boccaccio is famous for his Decameron, a collection of one hundred tales told by ten young people fleeing the Black Death in Florence.

In the modern era, Italian literature has continued to flourish, with writers like Luigi Pirandello, Italo Svevo, and Alberto Moravia exploring themes of existentialism, alienation, and the absurdity of modern life. Pirandello's plays, such as Six Characters in Search of an Author, challenged traditional notions of reality and identity, while Svevo's novel, Confessions of Zeno, delved into the complexities of human psychology and desire.

In the post-war period, Italian literature experienced a renaissance of sorts, with writers like Italo Calvino, Umberto Eco, and Elena Ferrante gaining international acclaim for their innovative and thought-provoking works. Calvino, in particular, is known for his playful and imaginative storytelling, blending elements of fantasy, science fiction, and philosophy in works like Invisible Cities and If on a winter's night a traveler.

Italian literature continues to evolve and adapt to the changing times, with a new generation of writers exploring themes of migration, identity, and globalization in works that reflect the complexities of contemporary Italian society. From the ancient epics of Dante to the postmodern fables of Calvino, Italian literature offers a rich and diverse tapestry of voices and perspectives that continue to captivate and inspire readers around the world.

Italian Cinema: Neorealism to Contemporary Masterpieces

Italian cinema is a vibrant and influential force in the world of film, with a rich history that spans from the neorealism movement of the mid-20th century to contemporary masterpieces that continue to captivate audiences around the globe. Neorealism, which emerged in Italy in the aftermath of World War II, sought to depict the harsh realities of post-war life with honesty and authenticity. Films like Roberto Rossellini's "Rome, Open City" and Vittorio De Sica's "Bicycle Thieves" captured the struggles of ordinary people living in poverty and adversity, paving the way for a new era of socially conscious filmmaking.

In the 1960s and 70s, Italian cinema experienced a period of artistic experimentation and innovation, with directors like Federico Fellini, Michelangelo Antonioni, and Luchino Visconti pushing the boundaries of cinematic storytelling and visual expression. Fellini's surreal and dreamlike films, such as "La Dolce Vita" and "8½," challenged conventional narrative structures and explored themes of alienation, desire, and the search for meaning in the modern world.

In the decades that followed, Italian cinema continued to evolve and adapt to changing tastes and trends, with directors like Bernardo Bertolucci,

Pier Paolo Pasolini, and Ermanno Olmi exploring new genres and styles while remaining true to their artistic vision. Bertolucci's epic films, such as "The Last Emperor" and "The Conformist," combined sweeping historical narratives with intimate character studies, earning him international acclaim and numerous awards.

In more recent years, Italian cinema has seen a resurgence of creativity and critical acclaim, with directors like Paolo Sorrentino, Matteo Garrone, and Nanni Moretti garnering attention for their bold and innovative storytelling. Sorrentino's "The Great Beauty," a lush and visually stunning meditation on art, beauty, and mortality set in contemporary Rome, won the Academy Award for Best Foreign Language Film in 2014, cementing his status as one of Italy's leading filmmakers.

Italian cinema continues to be celebrated for its distinct style, craftsmanship, and storytelling prowess, with a diverse range of genres and themes represented on screen. From gritty crime dramas and intimate character studies to lush historical epics and surreal fantasies, Italian filmmakers continue to push the boundaries of cinematic artistry and captivate audiences with their unique vision and storytelling flair.

Italian Festivals and Traditions: Celebrating Life Italian Style

Italian festivals and traditions are a vibrant reflection of the country's rich cultural heritage and zest for life. From ancient religious rituals to modern-day celebrations, Italians have a long history of coming together to mark special occasions and honor their traditions.

One of the most famous Italian festivals is Carnevale, a festive season that takes place in the weeks leading up to Lent. Originating in Venice in the Middle Ages, Carnevale is known for its elaborate masks, colorful costumes, and lively parades. Today, Carnevale celebrations can be found throughout Italy, with cities like Viareggio and Ivrea hosting some of the most extravagant and festive events.

Another beloved Italian tradition is the Feast of San Gennaro, celebrated in Naples each year on September 19th. The festival honors the city's patron saint, San Gennaro, with religious processions, street fairs, and culinary delights. The highlight of the festival is the Miracle of San Gennaro, when the saint's blood is said to liquefy in a vial kept in Naples Cathedral, a sign of good fortune for the city.

Italy is also famous for its rich culinary traditions, which are celebrated throughout the year with a variety of food festivals and events. From the truffle festivals of Alba to the olive oil festivals of Tuscany, Italians take great pride in their regional specialties and local ingredients, showcasing them in a variety of delicious dishes and culinary creations.

In addition to religious and culinary festivals, Italy also celebrates a number of secular holidays and traditions, such as Ferragosto, a public holiday that takes place on August 15th and marks the peak of the summer season. Italians typically spend Ferragosto at the beach or in the mountains, enjoying picnics, barbecues, and outdoor activities with family and friends.

Throughout the year, Italians also celebrate a number of traditional holidays and customs, such as Christmas, Easter, and La Festa della Repubblica, which commemorates the founding of the Italian Republic on June 2nd. These holidays are typically marked with special meals, gatherings, and rituals that bring families and communities together to celebrate and honor their shared heritage and traditions.

Overall, Italian festivals and traditions are a colorful and vibrant expression of the country's unique culture and history. Whether it's the elaborate costumes of Carnevale, the delicious flavors of a regional food festival, or the religious processions of San Gennaro, Italians know how to celebrate life with style, passion, and gusto.

La Dolce Vita: Italian Way of Life

La Dolce Vita, or "the sweet life," encapsulates the essence of the Italian way of life – a celebration of beauty, pleasure, and the simple joys of everyday living. From the bustling piazzas of Rome to the sun-drenched beaches of the Amalfi Coast, Italy is a country that embraces life with passion, warmth, and gusto.

At the heart of La Dolce Vita is the Italian appreciation for good food and wine. Italians take great pride in their culinary heritage, with each region boasting its own specialties and delicacies. From the hearty pasta dishes of the north to the fresh seafood of the south, Italian cuisine is as diverse as it is delicious, with an emphasis on quality ingredients, simple preparation, and shared meals with family and friends.

In addition to food, Italians also place a high value on personal relationships and social connections. Family is at the center of Italian life, with gatherings around the dinner table serving as an opportunity to bond, share stories, and reconnect with loved ones. Italians also have a strong sense of community, with neighbors and friends often coming together for festivals, celebrations, and spontaneous gatherings in the local piazza.

Italians also have a deep appreciation for beauty and aesthetics, evident in their love of art, architecture, and design. From the ancient ruins of Rome to the Renaissance masterpieces of Florence, Italy is a country that is rich in cultural heritage and artistic expression. Italians take pleasure in surrounding themselves with beauty, whether it's in the form of a well-crafted espresso, a beautifully tailored suit, or a carefully tended garden.

But perhaps the most defining aspect of La Dolce Vita is the Italian attitude toward life itself – a philosophy of living in the moment and savoring the small pleasures that make life worth living. Italians have a laid-back approach to time, with a greater emphasis on quality over quantity and a willingness to slow down and enjoy the moment. Whether it's lingering over a leisurely meal with friends, taking an afternoon passeggiata through the streets of Florence, or simply enjoying a glass of wine as the sun sets over the Tuscan countryside, Italians know how to appreciate the beauty and richness of life in all its forms.

Overall, La Dolce Vita is a celebration of all that is good and beautiful in life – a reminder to slow down, savor the moment, and appreciate the simple pleasures that surround us. In a world that often seems to move at breakneck speed, the Italian way of life offers a refreshing antidote – a reminder to stop and smell the roses, to treasure the moments of joy and connection that make life truly sweet.

Rome: The Eternal City

Rome, often referred to as the Eternal City, is one of the most iconic and historic cities in the world. Founded over two and a half millennia ago, Rome has played a central role in the development of Western civilization, serving as the capital of the Roman Empire and later as the seat of the Catholic Church. With its rich history, stunning architecture, and vibrant culture, Rome continues to captivate and inspire visitors from around the globe.

At the heart of Rome lies the ancient ruins of the Roman Forum, once the political, religious, and commercial center of the Roman Empire. Here, visitors can stroll among the ancient temples, basilicas, and government buildings that once stood at the heart of one of the greatest civilizations in history. Nearby, the Colosseum stands as a symbol of Rome's power and grandeur, a massive amphitheater where gladiators once fought for their lives before cheering crowds.

Rome is also home to some of the most iconic landmarks in the world, including the Vatican City, an independent city-state and the spiritual center of the Catholic Church. Here, visitors can marvel at the magnificent St. Peter's Basilica, with its towering dome and ornate façade, as well as the stunning Vatican Museums, home to some of the greatest works of art in history, including

Michelangelo's masterpiece, the Sistine Chapel ceiling.

But Rome is more than just ancient ruins and religious sites – it's also a vibrant and modern city, with bustling streets, lively piazzas, and a thriving culinary scene. Visitors can explore the charming neighborhoods of Trastevere and Monti, with their narrow cobblestone streets and colorful buildings, or sample the city's famous cuisine at one of its many trattorias, cafes, and gelaterias.

Rome is also a city of art and culture, with world-class museums, galleries, and theaters showcasing the best of Italian and international talent. From the stunning frescoes of the Capitoline Museums to the contemporary art exhibits at the MAXXI Museum, Rome offers something for every art lover to enjoy.

But perhaps the most magical thing about Rome is simply walking its streets and soaking in the atmosphere – the sense of history that seems to permeate every corner, the beauty of its architecture, and the warmth and hospitality of its people. Whether you're exploring the ancient ruins of the Forum, marveling at the grandeur of the Vatican, or simply enjoying a leisurely stroll along the Tiber River, Rome is a city that never fails to enchant and inspire.

Florence: Cradle of the Renaissance

Florence, known as the Cradle of the Renaissance, is a city steeped in history, art, and culture. Situated in the heart of Tuscany, Florence was a thriving center of commerce and trade during the Middle Ages, thanks to its strategic location along the Arno River and its proximity to the Mediterranean Sea. But it was during the Renaissance, in the 14th and 15th centuries, that Florence truly came into its own as one of the most important cultural and artistic centers in Europe.

The Renaissance, a period of rebirth and renewal, saw Florence become a hub of creativity and innovation, attracting some of the greatest artists, thinkers, and scholars of the time. Visionaries like Leonardo da Vinci, Michelangelo Buonarroti, and Sandro Botticelli flourished in Florence, creating masterpieces that would forever change the course of art history. From Michelangelo's iconic statue of David to Botticelli's ethereal paintings of Venus and Primavera, Florence's artistic legacy is unparalleled.

But Florence's influence extended beyond the realm of art – it was also a center of intellectual and scientific inquiry, with figures like Galileo

Galilei and Niccolò Machiavelli making significant contributions to their respective fields. Galileo's experiments with the telescope revolutionized our understanding of the cosmos, while Machiavelli's political treatise, The Prince, remains one of the most influential works of political philosophy ever written.

One of the most enduring symbols of Florence's Renaissance heritage is the Florence Cathedral, also known as the Duomo. With its magnificent dome designed by Filippo Brunelleschi, the Duomo is a masterpiece of Renaissance architecture and engineering, towering over the city skyline and serving as a testament to Florence's ambition and artistic prowess.

Florence is also home to some of the world's most renowned museums and galleries, including the Uffizi Gallery, which houses a vast collection of Renaissance art, and the Accademia Gallery, where Michelangelo's David resides. These institutions attract millions of visitors each year, eager to experience firsthand the beauty and brilliance of Florence's artistic treasures.

But Florence is more than just a museum – it's a living, breathing city, with a vibrant cultural scene, lively street markets, and bustling piazzas. Visitors can wander the winding streets of the historic center, stopping to admire the architecture of the Ponte Vecchio, browse the stalls of the San Lorenzo Market, or enjoy a leisurely meal at a traditional trattoria.

Today, Florence continues to be celebrated as a beacon of art, culture, and history, drawing visitors from around the world who come to experience the magic of the Renaissance firsthand. With its timeless beauty, rich heritage, and enduring legacy, Florence remains a testament to the power of human creativity and imagination.

Venice: City of Canals and Romance

Venice, often referred to as the City of Canals and Romance, is one of the most unique and enchanting cities in the world. Situated on a group of 118 small islands separated by canals and linked by bridges, Venice is a place like no other, with its picturesque waterways, historic palaces, and romantic ambiance.

The city's origins can be traced back over a thousand years, to the fall of the Western Roman Empire, when refugees fleeing barbarian invasions sought refuge in the marshy lagoon of the Adriatic Sea. Over time, these settlers built a network of canals, bridges, and buildings on the islands, creating the foundation for what would become one of the most powerful and prosperous cities in Europe.

Venice reached its peak of power and wealth during the Middle Ages and the Renaissance, when it was a major center of trade, commerce, and cultural exchange. The city's strategic location at the crossroads of the Mediterranean made it a hub of maritime trade, with merchants from all over the world flocking to its markets to buy and sell goods.

But Venice's wealth was not just material – it was also cultural and artistic. The city was home to some of the greatest artists, musicians, and thinkers of the time, including Titian, Tintoretto, and Vivaldi, who flourished under the patronage of the city's wealthy merchant families. The result was a flourishing of art, architecture, and music that left an indelible mark on the city and its inhabitants.

Today, Venice is perhaps best known for its iconic canals, which crisscross the city like a network of watery streets. Visitors can explore these canals by gondola or vaporetto, taking in the sights of historic palaces, churches, and bridges that line their shores. The Grand Canal, Venice's main thoroughfare, is lined with magnificent palaces and mansions, many of which date back to the city's heyday as a maritime republic.

But Venice is more than just canals and historic buildings – it's also a city of romance and intrigue, with its narrow streets and hidden alleyways providing the perfect backdrop for a romantic getaway. Couples can stroll hand in hand through the winding streets of the city, stopping to admire the views from the Rialto Bridge or enjoy a candlelit dinner in one of the city's many charming restaurants.

Despite its timeless beauty and allure, Venice faces challenges in the modern world, including rising sea levels, overcrowding, and the impact of mass tourism. But the city's residents are determined to preserve its unique heritage and way of life, working tirelessly to protect its historic buildings and cultural treasures for future generations to enjoy.

In the end, Venice remains a symbol of romance, beauty, and resilience – a city that continues to captivate and inspire all who visit it, with its timeless charm and unparalleled allure.

Milan: Fashion Capital of the World

Milan, the fashion capital of the world, is a city synonymous with style, sophistication, and innovation. Situated in the northern region of Lombardy, Milan is not only Italy's financial and commercial hub but also a global powerhouse in the fashion industry.

The city's reputation as a fashion mecca dates back centuries, with Milanese artisans and tailors renowned for their craftsmanship and attention to detail. In the Middle Ages, Milan was a center of textile production, with skilled artisans producing luxurious fabrics and garments for the nobility and elite.

But it was during the 20th century that Milan truly emerged as a fashion capital, thanks in part to the efforts of pioneering designers like Giorgio Armani, Gianni Versace, and Miuccia Prada. These designers revolutionized the fashion industry with their bold designs, innovative techniques, and uncompromising vision, catapulting Milan to the forefront of global fashion.

Today, Milan is home to some of the world's most prestigious fashion houses, including Gucci, Dolce & Gabbana, and Valentino, as well as countless up-and-coming designers and brands. Twice a year, the city plays host to Milan Fashion Week, one of the most important events on the fashion calendar, where designers showcase their latest collections to buyers, press, and fashionistas from around the world. But Milan's influence extends beyond the runway – the city is also a hub of creativity and culture, with a thriving arts scene, world-class museums, and architectural landmarks that reflect its rich history and heritage. Visitors to Milan can explore iconic sites like the Milan Cathedral, with its stunning Gothic architecture and intricate marble façade, or the historic La Scala opera house, where some of the world's greatest operas have premiered.

In addition to its fashion and cultural attractions, Milan is also a vibrant and dynamic city with a bustling nightlife, gourmet restaurants, and trendy neighborhoods like Brera and Navigli. Whether you're sipping an espresso in a chic café, browsing the latest collections in a designer boutique, or exploring the city's historic streets and landmarks, Milan offers something for everyone to enjoy.

In the end, Milan's status as the fashion capital of the world is a testament to its creativity, innovation, and entrepreneurial spirit. With its unique blend of tradition and modernity, style and substance, Milan continues to inspire and captivate fashion lovers around the globe, cementing its place as a global leader in the world of fashion and design.

Naples: Gateway to Southern Italy

Naples, often referred to as the Gateway to Southern Italy, is a city of contrasts, where ancient history meets modern life, and tradition blends seamlessly with innovation. Situated in the Campania region, Naples is the third-largest city in Italy and one of the oldest continuously inhabited cities in the world.

The city's history stretches back over two millennia, to its founding by the Greeks in the 8th century BC. Known as Neapolis, or "new city," Naples quickly grew into a thriving metropolis, serving as an important center of trade and culture in the ancient world. Over the centuries, Naples has been ruled by a succession of civilizations, including the Romans, Byzantines, Normans, and Spanish, each leaving their mark on the city's architecture, cuisine, and culture.

Today, Naples is a vibrant and bustling city, with a rich cultural heritage and a lively street life. Visitors to Naples can explore the city's historic center, a UNESCO World Heritage Site, with its narrow alleys, grand piazzas, and centuries-old churches and palaces. Highlights include the Duomo di San Gennaro, a magnificent cathedral dedicated to the city's patron saint, and the Royal Palace of Naples, a grand Bourbon-era palace with opulent interiors and beautiful gardens.

But Naples is more than just a city of history – it's also a city of art, with world-class museums and galleries showcasing the work of some of Italy's greatest artists. The National Archaeological Museum of Naples, one of the most important archaeological museums in the world, houses a vast collection of artifacts from ancient Greece, Rome, and Egypt, including the treasures of Pompeii and Herculaneum.

Naples is also famous for its culinary tradition, with dishes like pizza, spaghetti, and sfogliatella originating in the city and its surrounding region. Visitors can sample these delicious specialties at local trattorias, pizzerias, and street vendors, experiencing firsthand the bold flavors and fresh ingredients that characterize Neapolitan cuisine.

But perhaps the most iconic symbol of Naples is Mount Vesuvius, the active volcano that looms over the city and its bay. Despite the constant threat of eruption, Vesuvius has become a symbol of Naples' resilience and vitality, with locals and visitors alike marveling at its beauty and power.

In the end, Naples is a city of contradictions – ancient yet modern, chaotic yet charming, gritty yet glamorous. With its rich history, vibrant culture, and stunning natural beauty, Naples continues to captivate and inspire all who visit, serving as a gateway to the soul of Southern Italy.

Turin: Industrial Heartland and Chocolate Capital

Turin, nestled in the Piedmont region of northern Italy, is a city renowned for its rich industrial heritage and its status as the capital of chocolate. With a history that dates back over two thousand years, Turin has evolved from a Roman settlement to a thriving modern metropolis, while still preserving its unique cultural identity and traditions.

The city's industrial legacy can be traced back to the 19th century when Turin emerged as a major center of manufacturing and innovation. It was here that Italy's first railway was built, connecting Turin to the rest of the country and fueling the city's growth as an industrial powerhouse. Turin was also home to FIAT, one of Italy's largest and most iconic automotive companies, which played a central role in the city's industrial development.

Today, Turin's industrial past is still visible in its architecture, with grand boulevards, elegant squares, and stately palaces that reflect the city's prosperity during the industrial era. The Mole Antonelliana, originally built as a synagogue and now home to the National Museum of Cinema, stands as a symbol of Turin's industrial heritage, with its distinctive spire dominating the city skyline.

But Turin is perhaps best known as the chocolate capital of Italy, thanks to its long-standing tradition of chocolate-making and confectionery. The city's love affair with chocolate dates back to the 17th century when cocoa was first introduced to Europe from the New World. Turin's chocolatiers quickly embraced this new ingredient, creating delicious treats like gianduja, a smooth hazelnut chocolate spread, and gianduiotti, bite-sized chocolate pralines.

Today, Turin is home to some of Italy's most famous chocolate shops and cafes, where visitors can indulge in a decadent array of chocolates, pastries, and desserts. The city also hosts an annual chocolate festival, CioccolaTò, where chocolate lovers from around the world gather to celebrate their passion for all things chocolate.

But Turin offers more than just chocolate – it's also a city of culture, with world-class museums, galleries, and theaters showcasing the best of Italian and international art and entertainment. Visitors can explore the Royal Palace of Turin, a lavish Baroque palace that was once the residence of the House of Savoy, or admire the works of art at the Museo Egizio, one of the most important Egyptian museums in the world.

In addition to its cultural attractions, Turin is also a city of green spaces, with parks, gardens, and tree-lined boulevards that provide a welcome respite from the hustle and bustle of city life. The Parco del Valentino, with its riverside promenades and botanical gardens, is a favorite spot for locals and visitors alike to relax and unwind.

In the end, Turin's industrial heritage and chocolate-making tradition are just two facets of this vibrant and dynamic city. With its rich history, cultural attractions, and culinary delights, Turin continues to captivate and inspire all who visit, offering a taste of the good life in the heart of northern Italy.

Genoa: Birthplace of Christopher Columbus

Genoa, nestled along the rugged coastline of the Ligurian Sea, holds a significant place in history as the birthplace of one of the world's most famous explorers, Christopher Columbus. But beyond its association with the renowned explorer, Genoa boasts a rich maritime heritage, stunning architecture, and a vibrant cultural scene.

Founded by the ancient Ligurians, Genoa rose to prominence during the Middle Ages as a powerful maritime republic, dominating trade routes in the Mediterranean and beyond. Its strategic location along the Italian Riviera made it a key player in the spice and silk trades, fostering wealth and prosperity for its merchants and traders.

It was during this time that Genoa produced one of its most famous sons, Christopher Columbus, who would go on to change the course of history with his voyages to the New World. Born in the city in 1451, Columbus grew up amid the bustling port and maritime activity of Genoa, setting the stage for his later explorations and discoveries.

Today, visitors to Genoa can explore the city's historic center, a UNESCO World Heritage Site, with its winding medieval streets, grand palaces, and ancient churches. Highlights include the Palazzo Ducale, a magnificent palace that once served as the seat of the Doges of Genoa, and the Cathedral of San Lorenzo, a stunning example of Romanesque and Gothic architecture.

Genoa is also home to one of the largest and most important seaports in Italy, with a bustling harbor that serves as a gateway to the Mediterranean and beyond. The port of Genoa has played a central role in the city's history and economy, serving as a hub for trade, commerce, and industry for centuries.

In addition to its maritime heritage, Genoa is also a city of culture, with world-class museums, galleries, and theaters showcasing the best of Italian and international art and entertainment. Visitors can explore the Galata Maritime Museum, which tells the story of Genoa's seafaring history, or admire the works of art at the Palazzo Rosso and Palazzo Bianco.

But perhaps the most charming aspect of Genoa is its vibrant street life, with bustling markets, lively piazzas, and waterfront promenades where locals and visitors alike gather to enjoy the city's unique ambiance. Whether you're sipping an espresso in a cozy cafe, browsing the stalls of the Mercato Orientale, or simply strolling along the waterfront, Genoa offers a taste of authentic Italian life in a city steeped in history and tradition.

Palermo: Jewel of Sicily

Palermo, the Jewel of Sicily, exudes a captivating blend of history, culture, and Mediterranean charm. Nestled on the northern coast of the island, Palermo has been shaped by a rich tapestry of civilizations, from the ancient Greeks and Romans to the Arabs and Normans, each leaving their mark on the city's architecture, cuisine, and way of life.

One of Palermo's most iconic landmarks is the Norman Palace, a magnificent palace complex that was once the seat of Sicily's rulers. Built in the 9th century, the palace is renowned for its stunning mosaics, intricate architecture, and lush gardens, offering visitors a glimpse into Sicily's storied past.

Another must-visit attraction in Palermo is the Cathedral of Palermo, a grandiose structure that blends Norman, Arab, and Gothic styles. The cathedral's imposing facade and ornate interior make it a masterpiece of medieval architecture, while its royal tombs and historic crypts provide insight into the city's royal heritage.

But perhaps the most enchanting aspect of Palermo is its vibrant street life, with bustling markets, lively piazzas, and colorful neighborhoods that pulse with energy and vitality. Visitors can wander through the bustling stalls of the Ballarò market, sampling local delicacies like arancini and cannoli, or explore the maze-like streets of the historic Vucciria district, where hidden gems await around every corner.

Palermo is also a city of cultural richness, with world-class museums, galleries, and theaters showcasing the best of Sicilian art and heritage. The Palazzo Abatellis houses a remarkable collection of medieval and Renaissance art, while the Teatro Massimo, one of the largest opera houses in Europe, hosts performances by some of the world's most renowned artists and musicians.

Beyond its cultural attractions, Palermo is blessed with natural beauty, with stunning beaches, rugged mountains, and verdant valleys just a short drive away. Visitors can escape the hustle and bustle of the city and explore the pristine landscapes of the Madonie and Nebrodi mountain ranges, or relax on the sun-drenched shores of Mondello Beach, just a short distance from the city center.

In the end, Palermo's allure lies in its rich tapestry of history, culture, and natural beauty, offering visitors a truly immersive experience in the heart of Sicily. Whether you're exploring ancient ruins, savoring Sicilian cuisine, or simply soaking up the sun on a picturesque beach, Palermo promises an unforgettable journey through the soul of Sicily.

Bologna: Gastronomic Delights and Academic Hub

Bologna, nestled in the heart of the Emilia-Romagna region, is a city of gastronomic delights and academic excellence. Known affectionately as "La Grassa" (the fat one) for its culinary prowess and "La Dotta" (the learned one) for its prestigious university, Bologna offers visitors a unique blend of culinary traditions, cultural heritage, and intellectual vibrancy.

At the heart of Bologna's culinary scene is its world-renowned cuisine, which is characterized by its simplicity, freshness, and depth of flavor. The city is famous for its rich pasta dishes, such as tagliatelle al ragù (Bolognese sauce), tortellini in brodo (tortellini in broth), and lasagne alla Bolognese (Bolognese lasagna), all of which showcase the region's love affair with fresh pasta and savory sauces.

But Bologna's culinary delights extend far beyond pasta – the city is also known for its cured meats, cheeses, and traditional dishes like mortadella, parmigiano-reggiano, and crescentine fritte (fried dough balls). Visitors can sample these delicious specialties at local trattorias, osterias, and street markets, experiencing firsthand the rich flavors and culinary heritage of Bologna.

In addition to its gastronomic delights, Bologna is also a city of learning, with one of the oldest and most prestigious universities in Europe. Founded in 1088, the University of Bologna is renowned for its academic excellence and has produced some of Italy's greatest thinkers, artists, and scientists. Today, the university continues to attract students from around the world, contributing to the city's vibrant and diverse intellectual community.

But Bologna is more than just pasta and academia – it's also a city of architectural beauty, with a wealth of historic buildings, towers, and porticoes that reflect its rich cultural heritage. The city's historic center, with its medieval streets and elegant piazzas, is a UNESCO World Heritage Site, while landmarks like the Two Towers, the Basilica of San Petronio, and the Archiginnasio offer glimpses into Bologna's past and present.

Beyond its culinary and academic attractions, Bologna is also a city of cultural richness, with world-class museums, galleries, and theaters showcasing the best of Italian and international art and entertainment. Visitors can explore the collections at the National Art Gallery of

Bologna, attend a performance at the Teatro Comunale, or simply wander through the city's charming streets and squares, soaking up the vibrant atmosphere.

In the end, Bologna's blend of gastronomic delights, academic excellence, and cultural richness make it a truly unique destination in Italy. Whether you're indulging in a plate of fresh pasta, exploring the city's historic landmarks, or engaging in lively discussions with fellow students and scholars, Bologna promises an unforgettable experience for all who visit.

Verona: City of Romeo and Juliet

Verona, the City of Romeo and Juliet, is steeped in romance, history, and cultural significance. Located in the Veneto region of northern Italy, Verona is renowned for its association with Shakespeare's tragic love story, but its allure extends far beyond the realm of fiction.

One of the city's most iconic landmarks is Juliet's House, a 13th-century residence said to have inspired Shakespeare's tale of star-crossed lovers. Visitors flock to the house to see the famous balcony where Juliet is said to have declared her love for Romeo, as well as the courtyard adorned with love letters and messages from visitors around the world.

But Verona's connection to Romeo and Juliet is just one facet of its rich cultural heritage. The city boasts a wealth of historic buildings, churches, and monuments that reflect its long and storied past. Highlights include the Roman Arena, a magnificent amphitheater dating back to the 1st century AD, which still hosts opera performances and concerts to this day.

Verona is also home to a number of beautiful churches and basilicas, including the Basilica of San Zeno Maggiore, with its stunning Romanesque architecture and masterful frescoes. The city's historic center, with its winding medieval streets and elegant piazzas, is a UNESCO World Heritage Site, offering visitors a glimpse into Verona's rich architectural and artistic legacy.

In addition to its cultural attractions, Verona is also a city of natural beauty, with picturesque gardens, parks, and scenic viewpoints that offer breathtaking views of the city and surrounding countryside. The Giardino Giusti, with its manicured hedges and Renaissance-era sculptures, is a favorite spot for locals and visitors alike to relax and unwind.

Verona is also known for its vibrant cultural scene, with a calendar full of festivals, events, and performances throughout the year. The Verona Opera Festival, held annually in the Roman Arena, is one of the most prestigious opera events in the world, attracting opera lovers from around the globe.

But perhaps the most enchanting aspect of Verona is its timeless charm and romantic atmosphere, which can be felt in every corner of the city. Whether you're strolling hand in hand with your loved one along the Adige River, savoring a gelato in one of the city's quaint cafes, or admiring the sunset from the Ponte Pietra, Verona offers a truly magical experience for all who visit.

Pisa: Beyond the Leaning Tower

Pisa, a city in Tuscany, Italy, is famous worldwide for its iconic Leaning Tower, but there's much more to this historic city than its tilted landmark. Nestled along the banks of the Arno River, Pisa boasts a rich cultural heritage, stunning architecture, and a vibrant atmosphere that draws visitors from all corners of the globe.

The Leaning Tower of Pisa, constructed in the 12th century as a freestanding bell tower for the adjacent cathedral, is undoubtedly the city's most famous attraction. Its distinctive tilt, caused by unstable ground and poor foundation, has made it an enduring symbol of architectural marvel and human ingenuity. Visitors flock to Pisa to marvel at the tower's lean and climb its spiraling staircase for panoramic views of the city and surrounding countryside.

But beyond the Leaning Tower, Pisa is home to a wealth of historic landmarks and cultural treasures. The Piazza dei Miracoli, or Square of Miracles, is a UNESCO World Heritage Site and the heart of Pisa's architectural ensemble. In addition to the Leaning Tower, the square is also home to the Pisa Cathedral, a magnificent example of Romanesque architecture, and the Baptistery, with its exquisite marble facade and ornate interior.

Pisa's historic center is a labyrinth of narrow streets, bustling piazzas, and centuries-old buildings, where visitors can immerse themselves in the city's rich history and vibrant atmosphere. Highlights include the Piazza dei Cavalieri, once the political center of medieval Pisa and now home to the prestigious Scuola Normale Superiore, and the Palazzo Blu, a beautifully restored palace that houses a collection of modern and contemporary art.

Pisa is also a city of learning, with one of the oldest universities in Europe. Founded in 1343, the University of Pisa has produced some of Italy's greatest thinkers, scientists, and artists, contributing to the city's intellectual vibrancy and cultural diversity. Today, the university continues to attract students from around the world, adding to Pisa's dynamic and cosmopolitan atmosphere.

In addition to its cultural attractions, Pisa is also a city of natural beauty, with scenic parks, gardens, and riverside promenades that offer respite from the hustle and bustle of city life. Visitors can explore the lush landscapes of the Orto Botanico di Pisa, one of the oldest botanical gardens in Europe, or take a leisurely stroll along the Arno River, enjoying views of the city's historic landmarks and picturesque bridges.

In the end, Pisa's allure lies in its rich history, stunning architecture, and vibrant culture, making it a must-visit destination for travelers seeking to explore the beauty and charm of Tuscany. Whether you're admiring the Leaning Tower, wandering through the historic center, or savoring Tuscan cuisine in a local trattoria, Pisa promises an unforgettable experience for all who visit.

Siena: Home of the Palio Horse Race

Siena, a picturesque city in the heart of Tuscany, Italy, is renowned for its historic Palio horse race, a centuries-old tradition that captures the spirit and passion of the local community. But beyond the excitement of the Palio, Siena boasts a rich cultural heritage, stunning architecture, and a vibrant atmosphere that make it a truly unique destination for travelers.

The Palio di Siena, held twice a year on July 2nd and August 16th, is a thrilling horse race that pits the city's 17 contrade, or districts, against each other in a fierce competition for victory. The race takes place in the historic Piazza del Campo, the heart of Siena, where thousands of spectators gather to cheer on their favorite contrada and witness the pageantry and excitement of this ancient tradition.

But the Palio is just one aspect of Siena's rich cultural tapestry. The city is also home to a wealth of historic landmarks and artistic treasures that reflect its medieval past and Renaissance splendor. The Duomo di Siena, or Siena Cathedral, is a masterpiece of Gothic architecture, with its stunning facade, intricate marble floors, and magnificent dome. Inside, visitors can admire works of art by some of Italy's greatest artists, including Duccio di Buoninsegna and Donatello.

Siena's historic center, a UNESCO World Heritage Site, is a maze of narrow streets, hidden courtyards, and ancient palaces, where visitors can immerse themselves in the city's rich history and vibrant atmosphere. Highlights include the Palazzo Pubblico, a majestic palace that once served as the seat of Siena's government, and the Torre del Mangia, a towering medieval tower that offers panoramic views of the city and surrounding countryside.

In addition to its architectural treasures, Siena is also a city of cultural richness, with world-class museums, galleries, and theaters showcasing the best of Italian art and culture. The Museo dell'Opera del Duomo houses a remarkable collection of religious artifacts and sculptures, while the Pinacoteca Nazionale di Siena features works by Sienese artists from the Middle Ages to the Renaissance.

But perhaps the most enchanting aspect of Siena is its timeless charm and sense of community, which can be felt in every corner of the city. Whether you're savoring Tuscan cuisine in a cozy trattoria, exploring the winding streets of the historic center, or simply soaking up the atmosphere in a bustling piazza, Siena promises an unforgettable experience for all who visit.

Pompeii and Herculaneum: Cities Frozen in Time

Pompeii and Herculaneum, two ancient Roman cities nestled at the base of Mount Vesuvius in present-day Italy, are among the most famous archaeological sites in the world. Frozen in time by the catastrophic eruption of Mount Vesuvius in 79 AD, these cities offer a rare glimpse into daily life in ancient Rome.

The eruption of Mount Vesuvius buried Pompeii and Herculaneum under a thick layer of volcanic ash and debris, preserving buildings, artifacts, and even human remains in remarkable detail. Excavations began in the 18th century, uncovering a treasure trove of ancient artifacts and providing invaluable insights into Roman society, architecture, and culture.

Pompeii, the larger of the two cities, was a bustling commercial hub with a population of around 11,000 people at the time of the eruption. The city's well-preserved ruins include temples, forums, theaters, and villas, as well as the famous casts of victims caught in the throes of the disaster. Visitors can wander through Pompeii's ancient streets, marveling at the intricate frescoes, mosaic floors, and architectural marvels that offer a window into the past. Herculaneum, located just a few miles from Pompeii, was a smaller but equally prosperous city, with a population of around 4,000 people. The city's ruins are smaller in scale than Pompeii's but are remarkably well-preserved, offering a more intimate glimpse into Roman life. Highlights include the House of the Mosaic Atrium, with its stunning mosaic floors, and the Villa of the Papyri, home to one of the most extensive collections of ancient Roman scrolls ever discovered.

Both Pompeii and Herculaneum provide invaluable insights into various aspects of Roman life, including architecture, art, religion, and social structure. The artifacts uncovered at these sites have shed light on everything from Roman cuisine and fashion to politics and economics, enriching our understanding of this fascinating period in history.

Today, Pompeii and Herculaneum are UNESCO World Heritage Sites and major tourist attractions, drawing millions of visitors each year from around the world. Archaeologists continue to uncover new discoveries at these sites, further expanding our knowledge of ancient Rome and the impact of the Vesuvius eruption on the region.

In the end, Pompeii and Herculaneum stand as poignant reminders of the fragility of human civilization and the power of nature. Their well-preserved ruins offer a haunting glimpse into the past, allowing us to connect with the lives of those who lived and perished in the shadow of Mount Vesuvius nearly two millennia ago.

Cinque Terre: Coastal Charm and Colorful Villages

Cinque Terre, located on the rugged coastline of the Italian Riviera, is a collection of five picturesque villages that exude coastal charm and vibrant colors. Perched on steep cliffs overlooking the Ligurian Sea, these quaint villages – Monterosso al Mare, Vernazza, Corniglia, Manarola, and Riomaggiore – are connected by a network of hiking trails, scenic train rides, and winding coastal roads.

The name "Cinque Terre" translates to "Five Lands" in English, and each village has its own distinct character and charm. Monterosso al Mare, the largest and northernmost village, boasts sandy beaches, colorful umbrellas, and a lively waterfront promenade lined with cafes, restaurants, and shops. Vernazza, with its pastel-colored houses clustered around a small harbor, is often considered the most picturesque of the five villages, while Corniglia sits perched atop a rocky promontory, offering breathtaking views of the surrounding coastline.

Manarola and Riomaggiore, the southernmost villages, are known for their terraced vineyards, ancient stone buildings, and stunning sunsets. Visitors can explore the narrow alleys and hidden staircases of these villages, discovering hidden gems like local trattorias, artisanal shops, and family-run wineries.

One of the best ways to experience the beauty of Cinque Terre is by hiking along the Sentiero Azzurro, or Blue Trail, which winds its way along the coastline, offering panoramic views of the sea and surrounding countryside. The trail passes through each of the five villages, allowing hikers to immerse themselves in the natural beauty and cultural richness of the region.

In addition to hiking, visitors to Cinque Terre can also explore the villages by boat, kayak, or train, stopping to swim in secluded coves, sample fresh seafood and pesto, or simply soak up the laid-back atmosphere of coastal life. The region is also famous for its local specialties, including anchovies, focaccia, and Sciacchetrà wine, which can be enjoyed at waterfront cafes and trattorias overlooking the sea.

Cinque Terre has long been a favorite destination for travelers seeking to escape the hustle and bustle of city life and immerse themselves in the beauty of the Italian Riviera. Whether you're hiking along the coastal trails, lounging on the beach, or savoring the flavors of Ligurian cuisine, Cinque Terre promises an unforgettable experience for all who visit.

Amalfi Coast: Cliffside Beauty and Mediterranean Bliss

The Amalfi Coast, a stunning stretch of coastline in southern Italy, is renowned for its cliffside beauty, charming villages, and Mediterranean bliss. Nestled between the rugged cliffs of the Lattari Mountains and the azure waters of the Tyrrhenian Sea, this UNESCO World Heritage Site is a paradise for travelers seeking sun, sea, and relaxation.

The Amalfi Coast is named after the town of Amalfi, one of its most famous and historic villages. Founded by the Romans in the 9th century, Amalfi was once a powerful maritime republic and a major trading center in the Mediterranean. Today, visitors can explore the town's ancient streets, marvel at its stunning cathedral, and soak up the laid-back atmosphere of its picturesque waterfront.

But Amalfi is just one of many gems along the coast. The Amalfi Coast is also home to a number of other charming villages, each with its own unique character and allure. Positano, with its pastel-colored houses cascading down the cliffside, is perhaps the most iconic of these villages, attracting artists, writers, and celebrities from around the world.

Ravello, perched high above the coast, offers breathtaking views of the sea and surrounding countryside, as well as a rich cultural heritage that includes historic villas, lush gardens, and world-class music festivals. Other notable villages along the coast include Sorrento, known for its lemon groves and panoramic views of Mount Vesuvius, and Maiori, with its long sandy beach and bustling promenade. In addition to its charming villages, the Amalfi Coast is also famous for its natural beauty and scenic vistas. Visitors can explore the coastline by boat, kayak, or ferry, stopping to swim in hidden coves, snorkel among colorful marine life, or simply admire the dramatic cliffs and crystal-clear waters from the shore.

The Amalfi Coast is also a paradise for food lovers, with an abundance of fresh seafood, locally grown produce, and traditional dishes that showcase the flavors of the Mediterranean. From fresh-caught fish and seafood risotto to homemade limoncello and gelato, the cuisine of the Amalfi Coast is as delightful as its scenery.

Whether you're exploring historic villages, lounging on sun-drenched beaches, or savoring the flavors of Italian cuisine, the Amalfi Coast offers a truly magical experience for all who visit. With its cliffside beauty, Mediterranean bliss, and timeless charm, it's no wonder that the Amalfi Coast is considered one of the most beautiful destinations in the world.

Capri: Island Paradise in the Tyrrhenian Sea

Capri, a small island in the Tyrrhenian Sea off the coast of Naples, Italy, is a true paradise known for its breathtaking beauty, turquoise waters, and glamorous atmosphere. This idyllic island has captured the hearts of travelers for centuries, drawing visitors with its stunning landscapes, rich history, and luxurious lifestyle.

The island of Capri is famous for its rugged coastline, dramatic cliffs, and hidden coves, which offer endless opportunities for exploration and adventure. One of the most iconic landmarks on the island is the Faraglioni, three towering sea stacks that rise majestically from the sea and are a symbol of Capri's natural beauty. Visitors can admire the Faraglioni from land or sea, either by boat tour or hiking along the scenic coastal paths.

Capri's main town, also called Capri, is a charming maze of narrow streets, whitewashed buildings, and bustling piazzas, where visitors can stroll, shop, and soak up the island's vibrant atmosphere. The town is home to designer boutiques, chic cafes, and elegant restaurants, as well as historic landmarks like the Gardens of Augustus, which offer panoramic views of the sea and surrounding cliffs.

Another must-visit destination on Capri is the town of Anacapri, located at a higher elevation on the island's western side. Anacapri is known for its relaxed vibe, picturesque streets, and stunning views of the Gulf of Naples. Visitors can take a scenic chairlift ride to the top of Mount Solaro, the highest point on the island, for panoramic views of Capri and the surrounding coastline.

In addition to its natural beauty, Capri is also rich in history and culture. The island has been inhabited since ancient times and is home to several archaeological sites, including the ruins of Villa Jovis, the former palace of the Roman Emperor Tiberius. Visitors can explore the villa's ruins and learn about its fascinating history as a retreat for Roman emperors.

Capri is also famous for its glamorous lifestyle, attracting celebrities, artists, and jet-setters from around the world. The island's luxury hotels, exclusive beach clubs, and vibrant nightlife scene make it a popular destination for those seeking a taste of la dolce vita, or the sweet life.

Whether you're lounging on a sun-drenched beach, exploring ancient ruins, or sipping cocktails at a chic waterfront bar, Capri offers a truly unforgettable experience for all who visit. With its stunning scenery, rich history, and luxurious amenities, it's no wonder that Capri is considered one of the most beautiful and glamorous destinations in the world.

The Italian Alps: Majestic Mountains and Alpine Adventures

The Italian Alps, a majestic mountain range in northern Italy, offer breathtaking landscapes, thrilling outdoor adventures, and a rich cultural heritage. Stretching across the regions of Piedmont, Lombardy, Trentino-Alto Adige, and Veneto, the Italian Alps are a paradise for outdoor enthusiasts and nature lovers alike.

At the heart of the Italian Alps is the Dolomites, a UNESCO World Heritage Site renowned for its dramatic peaks, rugged terrain, and stunning rock formations. The Dolomites are a haven for hikers, climbers, and skiers, with thousands of miles of trails and slopes to explore. Visitors can hike through lush valleys, scale towering peaks, and marvel at panoramic views of the surrounding mountains and valleys.

In addition to its natural beauty, the Italian Alps are also home to charming alpine villages, historic towns, and cultural landmarks. The town of Cortina d'Ampezzo, known as the "Queen of the Dolomites," is a popular destination for winter sports enthusiasts, with world-class ski resorts, luxury hotels, and chic boutiques. Other notable towns in the region include Bolzano, with its mix of Italian and Austrian influences, and Merano, known for its thermal baths and Mediterranean climate.

The Italian Alps are also rich in history and culture, with a heritage that spans thousands of years. The region was inhabited by ancient tribes, including the Celts and the Romans, who left behind a wealth of archaeological sites and artifacts. Visitors can explore ancient ruins, medieval castles, and charming churches, learning about the region's fascinating past and cultural traditions.

One of the most iconic landmarks in the Italian Alps is the Matterhorn, a towering peak straddling the border between Italy and Switzerland. The Matterhorn is a symbol of the Alps and a popular destination for climbers and mountaineers, with its challenging routes and stunning views.

In addition to hiking and skiing, the Italian Alps offer a wide range of outdoor activities, including mountain biking, paragliding, and whitewater rafting. The region is also known for its culinary delights, with hearty alpine cuisine featuring locally sourced ingredients such as cheese, cured meats, and polenta.

Whether you're seeking adrenaline-pumping adventures or peaceful moments surrounded by nature, the Italian Alps offer something for everyone. With its majestic mountains, picturesque villages, and rich cultural heritage, the Italian Alps are a destination not to be missed.

Italian Lakes: Tranquility and Natural Splendor

Nestled amidst the rolling hills and picturesque landscapes of northern Italy lie the Italian Lakes, a collection of stunning bodies of water that have captivated travelers for centuries. Known for their tranquil beauty and natural splendor, the Italian Lakes offer a peaceful retreat from the hustle and bustle of everyday life.

The most famous of the Italian Lakes is Lake Como, a glacial lake nestled between the towering Alps and lush forests of Lombardy. With its sparkling blue waters, charming lakeside villages, and elegant villas, Lake Como has long been a favorite destination for celebrities, artists, and aristocrats. Visitors can explore historic towns like Bellagio, known as the "Pearl of Lake Como," with its cobbled streets, flower-filled gardens, and stunning views of the lake and surrounding mountains.

Lake Garda, the largest lake in Italy, is another popular destination in the Italian Lakes region. Surrounded by olive groves, lemon orchards, and vineyards, Lake Garda offers a diverse landscape of rugged cliffs, sandy beaches, and quaint villages. Visitors can explore historic towns like Sirmione, with its ancient Roman ruins and thermal baths, or take a boat cruise to the charming island of Isola del Garda, home to a stunning neo-Gothic villa and lush gardens.

Lake Maggiore, located on the border between Italy and Switzerland, is renowned for its Mediterranean climate, lush vegetation, and stunning islands. The Borromean Islands, a group of picturesque islets in the middle of the lake, are a must-visit destination, with their ornate palaces, botanical gardens, and colorful villages. Visitors can explore the islands by boat, stopping to admire the opulent interiors of the palaces or stroll through the manicured gardens.

In addition to their natural beauty, the Italian Lakes are also known for their outdoor recreational opportunities. Visitors can enjoy a wide range of activities, including sailing, windsurfing, hiking, and cycling, as well as wine tasting, shopping, and dining in the charming lakeside towns.

The Italian Lakes region is also rich in history and culture, with a wealth of historic landmarks, art museums, and cultural festivals to explore. Whether you're admiring the frescoes of the Villa Carlotta, wandering the streets of medieval villages like Varenna or Orta San Giulio, or simply relaxing on the shores of the lake, the Italian Lakes offer a tranquil and unforgettable experience for all who visit.

Tuscany: Rolling Hills and Chianti Vineyards

Tuscany, the heart of Italy, is a region of unparalleled beauty, renowned for its rolling hills, picturesque landscapes, and world-famous Chianti vineyards. Nestled in central Italy, Tuscany is a destination that embodies the essence of la dolce vita, or the sweet life, with its stunning countryside, rich history, and exquisite cuisine.

The rolling hills of Tuscany are perhaps its most iconic feature, dotted with charming hilltop towns, medieval castles, and centuries-old vineyards. Driving through the Tuscan countryside, one is greeted with vistas of endless vineyards, olive groves, and cypress trees, creating a timeless and idyllic landscape that has inspired artists, writers, and travelers for centuries.

At the heart of Tuscany lies the Chianti wine region, famous for its bold red wines and scenic vineyards. The area is home to some of Italy's most prestigious wineries, where visitors can tour the cellars, sample the wines, and learn about the winemaking process. The medieval town of Greve in Chianti serves as the gateway to the region, with its historic piazza, artisan shops, and weekly market showcasing local produce and crafts.

In addition to its wine, Tuscany is also known for its rich culinary tradition, with dishes that celebrate the region's bounty of fresh ingredients. From hearty ribollita soup and succulent bistecca alla fiorentina to delicate pici pasta and creamy gelato, Tuscan cuisine is a feast for the senses, reflecting the region's agricultural heritage and deep connection to the land.

Tuscany is also home to some of Italy's most famous cities and cultural treasures, including Florence, Siena, and Pisa. Florence, the capital of Tuscany, is renowned for its Renaissance art and architecture, with iconic landmarks such as the Duomo, the Uffizi Gallery, and the Ponte Vecchio drawing millions of visitors each year. Siena, with its medieval streets and historic palaces, is famous for its annual Palio horse race, while Pisa is known for its iconic Leaning Tower and magnificent Piazza dei Miracoli.

But beyond its cities and vineyards, Tuscany is a region of hidden gems and undiscovered treasures, where visitors can explore charming hilltop villages, ancient Etruscan ruins, and breathtaking natural wonders. Whether you're admiring the sunset over the rolling hills, sipping wine in a rustic farmhouse, or strolling through a medieval town, Tuscany offers a truly magical experience that will stay with you long after you've left.

Umbria: Italy's Green Heart

Nestled in the heart of Italy lies Umbria, a region known as Italy's Green Heart for its lush landscapes, rolling hills, and pristine natural beauty. While often overshadowed by its more famous neighbor, Tuscany, Umbria boasts a charm and tranquility all its own, attracting visitors with its picturesque countryside, medieval towns, and rich cultural heritage.

Umbria is characterized by its verdant hills, fertile valleys, and dense forests, making it a paradise for outdoor enthusiasts and nature lovers. The region is home to several national parks and nature reserves, including the Monti Sibillini National Park, which offers hiking trails, mountain biking routes, and opportunities for wildlife spotting. Visitors can explore the park's rugged peaks, sparkling lakes, and ancient beech forests, immersing themselves in the region's pristine natural landscapes.

In addition to its natural beauty, Umbria is also known for its charming hilltop towns and historic villages, each with its own unique character and cultural heritage. Perched atop hills overlooking the countryside, towns like Assisi, Spoleto, and Orvieto are steeped in history, with medieval streets, ancient churches, and well-preserved fortifications. Assisi, birthplace of St. Francis, is home to the stunning Basilica of St. Francis, a

UNESCO World Heritage Site renowned for its frescoes by Giotto and Cimabue.

Umbria is also famous for its culinary delights, with a cuisine that celebrates the region's abundance of fresh, local ingredients. Umbrian cuisine is characterized by its simplicity and authenticity, with dishes that showcase the region's rich agricultural heritage. Visitors can sample traditional dishes like porchetta, wild boar stew, and lentil soup, as well as local specialties such as truffles, olive oil, and cured meats.

Throughout Umbria, visitors will encounter a rich tapestry of art, history, and culture, from the ancient Roman ruins of Spoleto to the medieval palaces of Gubbio. The region is home to numerous festivals and events celebrating its cultural heritage, including the Umbria Jazz Festival in Perugia, one of the largest jazz festivals in the world, and the Festival dei Due Mondi in Spoleto, a renowned performing arts festival.

Whether exploring the region's historic towns, hiking through its scenic landscapes, or savoring its delicious cuisine, Umbria offers a truly unforgettable experience for all who visit. With its green hills, historic villages, and warm hospitality, Umbria invites travelers to slow down, relax, and immerse themselves in the timeless beauty of Italy's Green Heart.

Sicily: Mediterranean Melting Pot

Sicily, the largest island in the Mediterranean Sea, is a captivating blend of cultures, landscapes, and flavors, earning it the title of a Mediterranean melting pot. Located just off the southern coast of Italy, Sicily has been shaped by a rich tapestry of influences over the centuries, from ancient civilizations to medieval kingdoms to modern-day migrations.

The island's strategic location at the crossroads of Europe, Africa, and the Middle East has made it a coveted prize throughout history, with numerous civilizations leaving their mark on its shores. The Greeks, Romans, Arabs, Normans, and Spanish have all ruled Sicily at various points, each contributing to its unique cultural heritage.

One of the most enduring legacies of Sicily's diverse history is its architecture, which reflects the influence of its many conquerors. Visitors to Sicily can explore ancient Greek temples, Roman amphitheaters, Moorish palaces, Norman cathedrals, and Baroque churches, all within a single island. The historic city of Palermo, with its bustling markets, winding streets, and vibrant mix of architectural styles, is a testament to Sicily's multicultural past. Sicily's cultural heritage is also evident in its cuisine, which is a fusion of Mediterranean flavors and traditions. From arancini and caponata to cannoli and granita,

Sicilian cuisine is a feast for the senses, with dishes that showcase the island's bounty of fresh seafood, citrus fruits, olive oil, and spices. The island is also famous for its wines, particularly Marsala and Nero d'Avola, which are produced in vineyards that dot the countryside.

In addition to its rich history and culinary delights, Sicily is blessed with stunning natural beauty, including rugged coastlines, sandy beaches, and towering mountains. The island is home to Mount Etna, one of the most active volcanoes in the world, which dominates the eastern coast with its smoking crater and lava flows. The Aeolian Islands, a volcanic archipelago off the northern coast of Sicily, are a UNESCO World Heritage Site known for their dramatic landscapes and crystal-clear waters.

Sicily is also a land of ancient traditions and vibrant festivals, with celebrations that date back centuries. From the religious processions of Holy Week to the colorful carnivals of Carnevale, Sicilian festivals are a lively mix of music, dance, and pageantry, offering visitors a glimpse into the island's rich cultural heritage.

Whether exploring its historic sites, indulging in its delicious cuisine, or simply soaking up the sun on its beautiful beaches, Sicily offers a truly unforgettable experience for travelers seeking a taste of the Mediterranean's diverse and fascinating history.

The Italian Riviera: Sun, Sea, and Style

The Italian Riviera, stretching along the northwestern coast of Italy, is a paradise of sun, sea, and style that has captivated travelers for generations. With its stunning coastline, glamorous resorts, and charming seaside towns, the Italian Riviera offers a quintessentially Mediterranean experience that is both luxurious and laid-back.

At the heart of the Italian Riviera lies the Ligurian coast, home to some of the region's most iconic destinations, including the glamorous towns of Portofino and Santa Margherita Ligure. These picturesque villages, with their pastel-colored buildings, bustling harbors, and exclusive boutiques, have long been favored by celebrities, artists, and jet-setters seeking a taste of la dolce vita.

Further west, the Cinque Terre, a UNESCO World Heritage Site, offers a more rugged and unspoiled coastline, with five charming villages perched precariously on cliffs overlooking the sea. Visitors to the Cinque Terre can explore narrow cobblestone streets, vineyard-covered hillsides, and scenic hiking trails that wind along the rugged coastline, offering breathtaking views of the Mediterranean.

The Italian Riviera is also known for its beautiful beaches, which range from sandy stretches lined with sun loungers and umbrellas to secluded coves hidden among rocky cliffs. Popular beach destinations include Alassio, with its wide sandy beach and lively promenade, and Sanremo, known for its elegant seaside resorts and vibrant cultural scene.

In addition to its natural beauty, the Italian Riviera is also famous for its culinary delights, with a cuisine that celebrates the region's fresh seafood, olive oil, and aromatic herbs. Visitors can sample traditional Ligurian dishes such as pesto alla genovese, focaccia, and seafood risotto, as well as indulge in gelato, pastries, and other sweet treats.

Throughout the Italian Riviera, visitors will encounter a rich cultural heritage, with historic landmarks, art galleries, and museums showcasing the region's fascinating history and artistic legacy. From the medieval Old Town of Genoa to the glamorous casinos of Monte Carlo, the Italian Riviera offers a wealth of experiences for travelers seeking sun, sea, and style along the Mediterranean coast.

Exploring Italy: Practical Tips for Travelers

Embarking on a journey to Italy is an exciting endeavor, filled with the promise of ancient wonders, mouthwatering cuisine, and unforgettable experiences. However, like any travel adventure, exploring Italy requires careful planning and consideration to ensure a smooth and enjoyable trip. Whether you're a seasoned traveler or venturing abroad for the first time, here are some practical tips to help you make the most of your Italian adventure.

First and foremost, it's essential to research and familiarize yourself with Italy's cultural customs, etiquette, and local customs. Italians are known for their warm hospitality and friendly demeanor, but it's important to show respect for their traditions and way of life. Learning a few basic Italian phrases, such as greetings and common courtesy expressions, can go a long way in fostering positive interactions with locals and enhancing your overall travel experience.

When it comes to packing for your trip, less is often more. Italy's diverse landscapes and climates, ranging from the sunny beaches of the Amalfi Coast to the snowy peaks of the Italian Alps, necessitate a versatile wardrobe that can adapt to changing conditions. Comfortable walking shoes are a must, as you'll likely be exploring historic cities and cobblestone streets on foot. Additionally, be sure to pack appropriate attire for visiting churches, museums, and other religious sites, which may have strict dress codes requiring modest clothing.

Navigating Italy's transportation network can be a breeze with a bit of preparation. The country boasts an extensive network of trains, buses, and ferries, making it easy to travel between cities and regions. Purchasing a rail pass or regional transportation card can offer significant savings and flexibility for exploring Italy's attractions. If you plan to drive, be aware of Italy's traffic laws, road signs, and driving customs, and consider renting a GPS or using a navigation app to help you navigate unfamiliar roads.

When it comes to dining in Italy, prepare to indulge in a culinary journey like no other. Italian cuisine is celebrated for its fresh, seasonal ingredients, simple yet flavorful dishes, and regional specialties. Don't be afraid to venture beyond the tourist hotspots and seek out authentic trattorias and osterias frequented by locals. And of course, no trip to Italy would be complete without sampling gelato, pizza, pasta, and other iconic Italian delicacies.

Finally, don't forget to savor the moment and embrace the Italian concept of "la dolce vita" – the sweet life. Take time to slow down, soak in the sights and sounds of Italy's vibrant cities and charming villages, and savor the simple pleasures of daily life, whether it's enjoying a leisurely cappuccino at a sidewalk cafe or watching the sunset over the Mediterranean Sea. With a spirit of adventure and a willingness to embrace the unexpected, your journey through Italy is sure to be an unforgettable experience.

Epilogue

In the grand tapestry of Italy, every corner tells a story, every cobblestone whispers of centuries gone by, and every dish served is a celebration of tradition and innovation. As we come to the end of our journey through this enchanting land, it's only fitting to reflect on the richness and diversity that make Italy truly timeless.

From the ancient ruins of Rome to the Renaissance masterpieces of Florence, from the sun-kissed beaches of the Amalfi Coast to the snow-capped peaks of the Italian Alps, Italy's landscapes are as varied as they are breathtaking. But it's not just the physical beauty of Italy that leaves a lasting impression – it's the people, the culture, and the spirit of the country that truly capture the heart.

Italy's cultural legacy is unparalleled, with contributions to art, music, literature, and cuisine that have shaped the course of human history. From Leonardo da Vinci to Dante Alighieri, from Vivaldi to Verdi, from Michelangelo to Modigliani, Italy has been home to some of the world's greatest artists, thinkers, and innovators. And its culinary heritage – from pizza and pasta to gelato and espresso – has become a global phenomenon, beloved by food lovers around the world.

But perhaps what makes Italy most special is its ability to embrace the old and the new, the past and the present, in perfect harmony. In Italy, ancient ruins stand side by side with modern skyscrapers, centuries-old traditions coexist with cutting-edge innovation, and the spirit of the Renaissance lives on in the bustling streets of its cities and towns.

As we bid arrivederci to Italy, let us carry with us the memories of its beauty, its history, and its warmth. And let us remember that Italy is not just a place on a map – it's a state of mind, a way of life, and a source of inspiration for generations to come. Grazie mille, Italia, for sharing your wonders with the world. Until we meet again.

Made in the USA
Middletown, DE
13 December 2024

66902338R00066